easy piano

michael
bublé
christmas

ISBN 978-1-4768-1199-4

HAL•LEONARD®
CORPORATION
7777 W. BLUEMOUND RD. P.O. BOX 13819 MILWAUKEE, WI 53213

Visit Hal Leonard Online at
www.halleonard.com

IT'S BEGINNING TO LOOK LIKE CHRISTMAS

By MEREDITH WILLSON

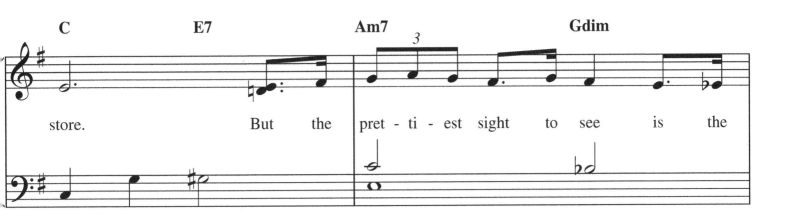

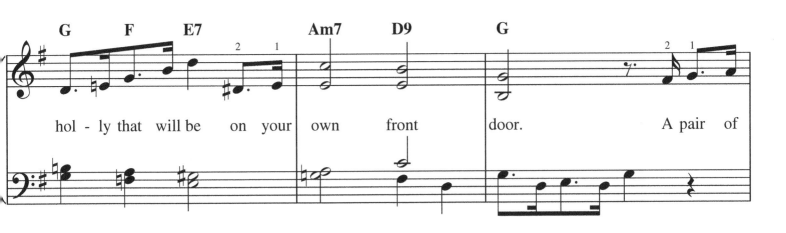

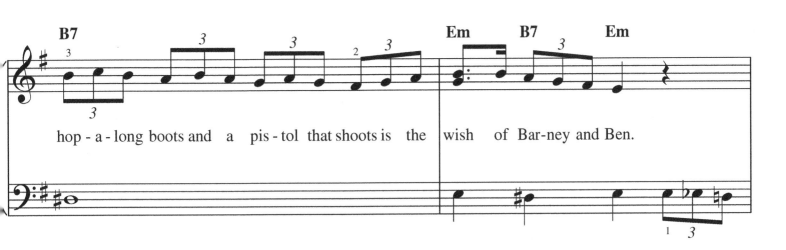

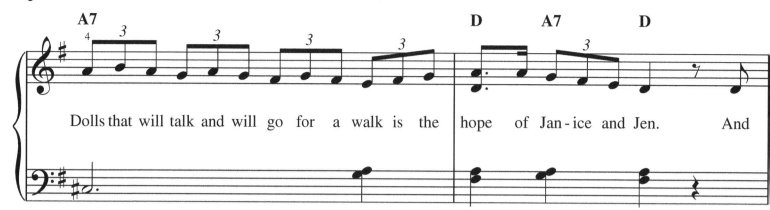

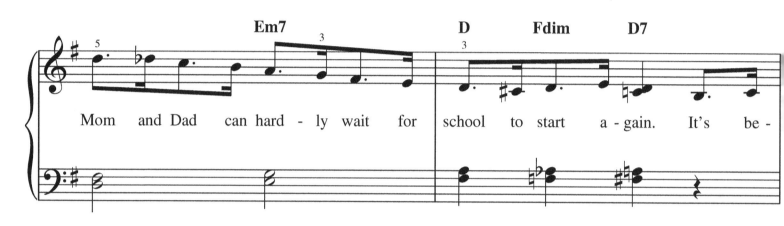

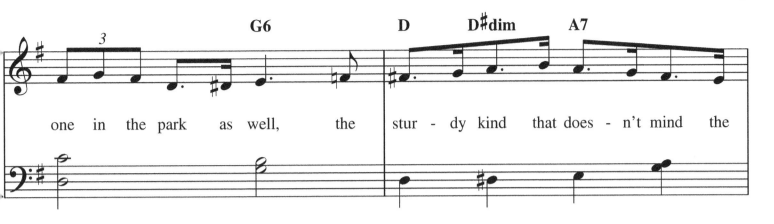

one in the park as well, the stur - dy kind that does - n't mind the

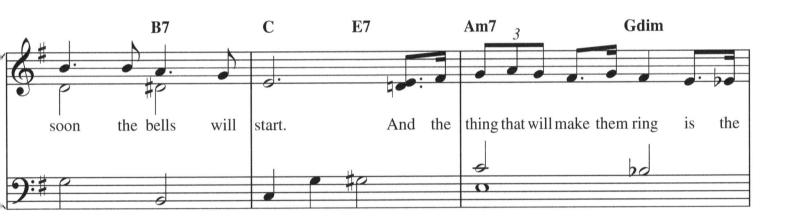

snow._____ It's be - gin-ning to look a lot like Christ - mas,

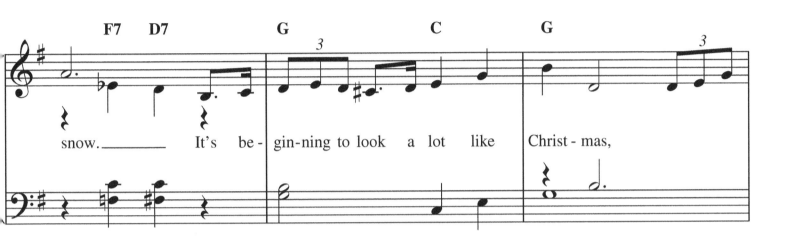

soon the bells will start. And the thing that will make them ring is the

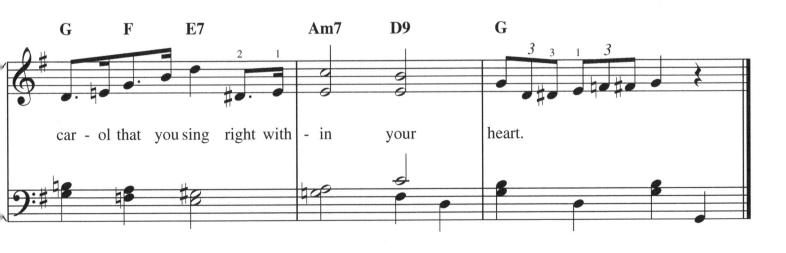

car - ol that you sing right with - in your heart.

SANTA CLAUS IS COMIN' TO TOWN

Words by HAVEN GILLESPIE
Music by J. FRED COOTS

You bet-ter watch out, you

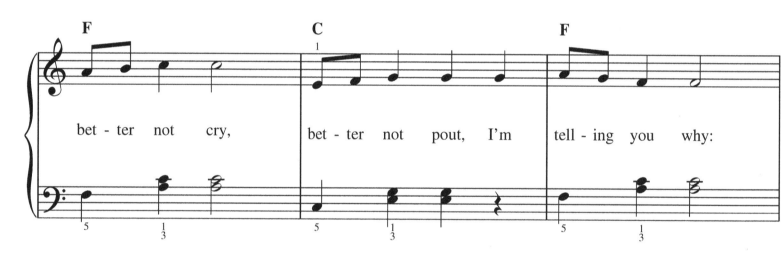

bet-ter not cry, bet-ter not pout, I'm tell-ing you why:

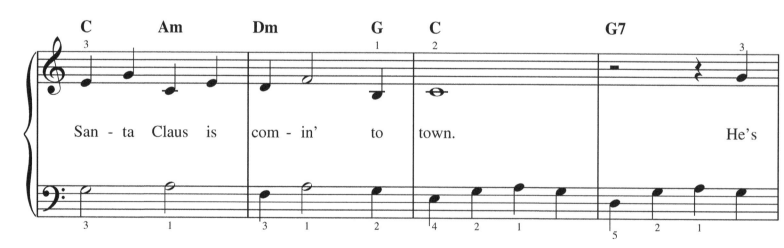

San-ta Claus is com-in' to town. He's

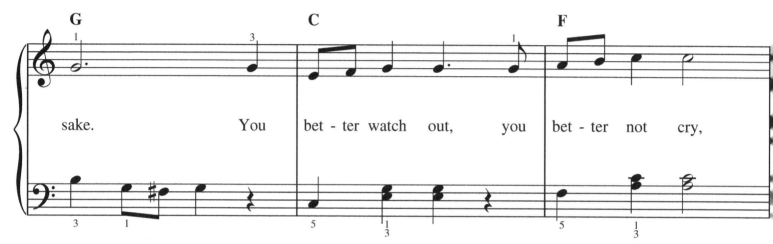

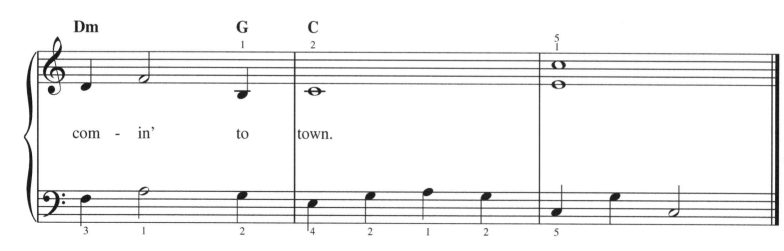

JINGLE BELLS

By JAMES PIERPONT

Arranged by David Foster, Patty Andrews and Victor Schoen

12

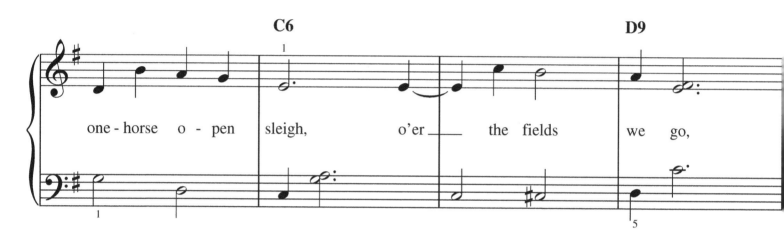

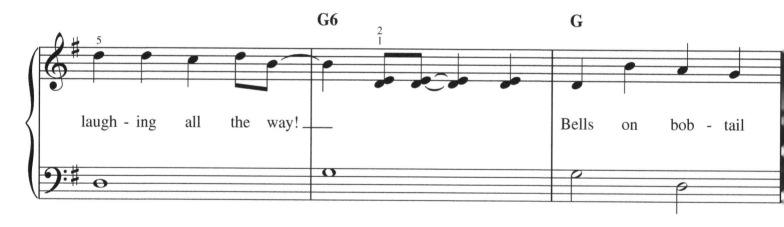

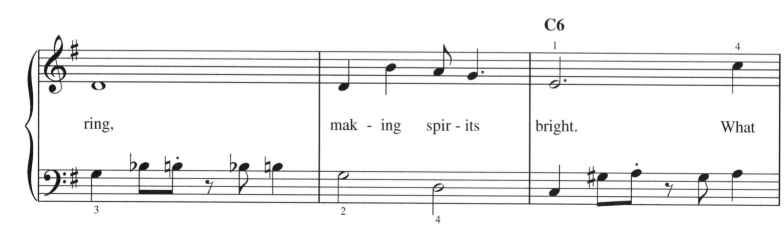

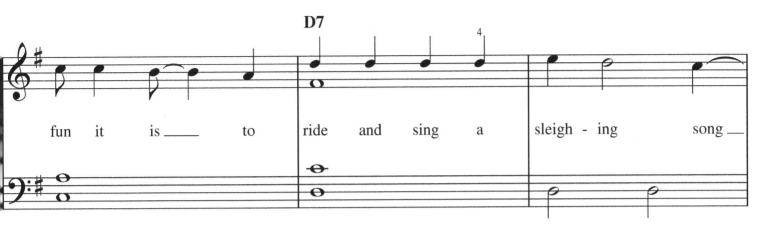

fun it is ___ to ride and sing a sleigh - ing song ___

___ to - night! Jin - gle ___ bells, ___ j - jin - gle ___

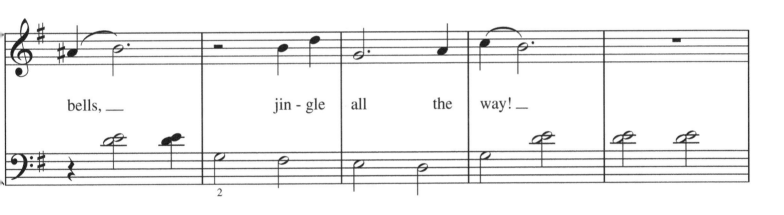

bells, ___ jin - gle all the way! ___

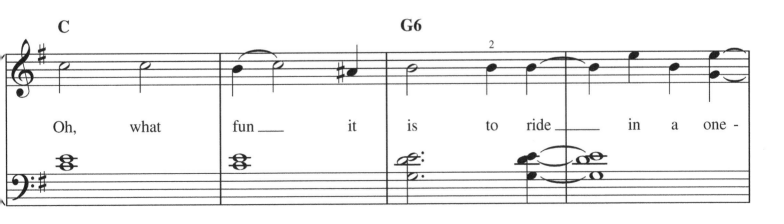

Oh, what fun ___ it is to ride ___ in a one -

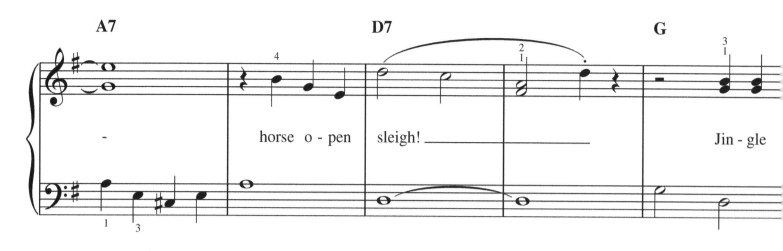

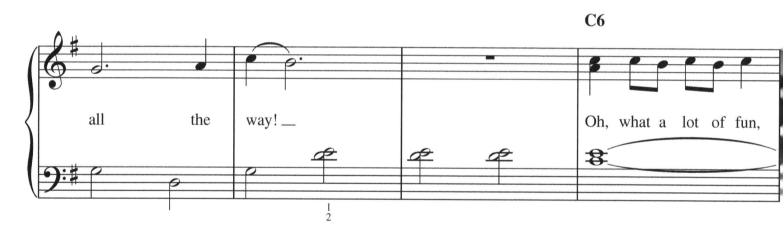

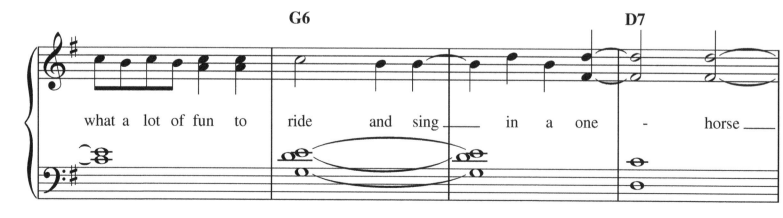

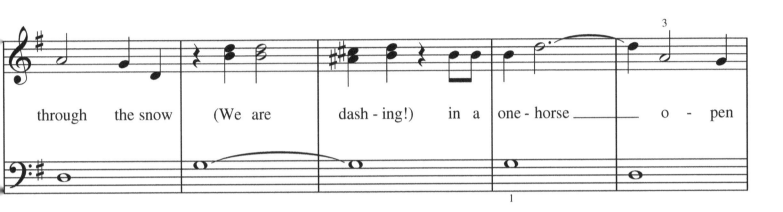

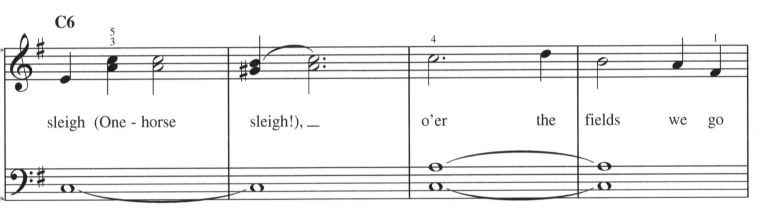

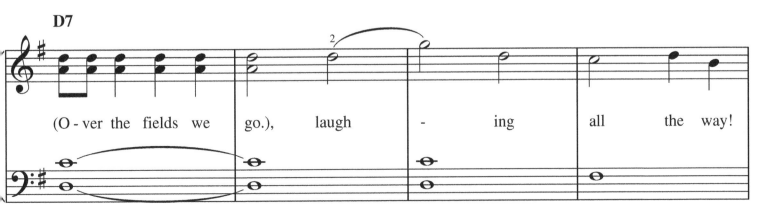

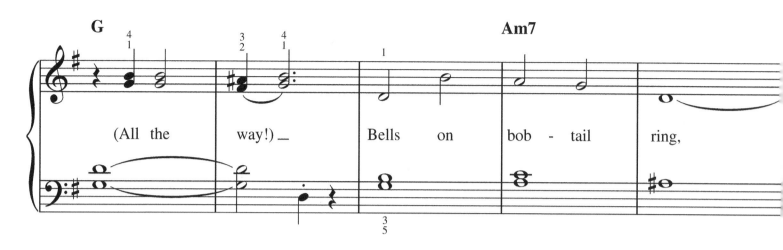

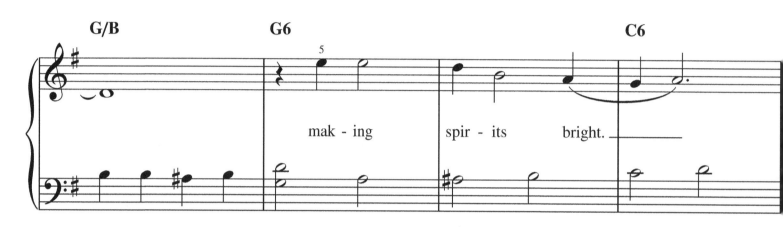

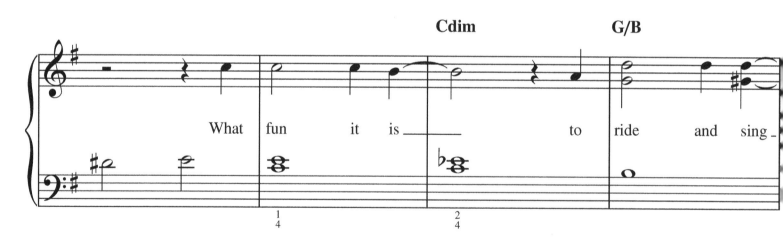

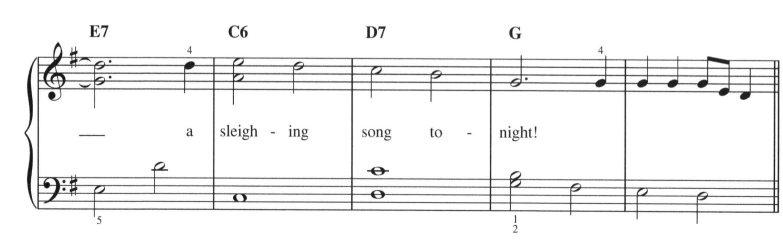

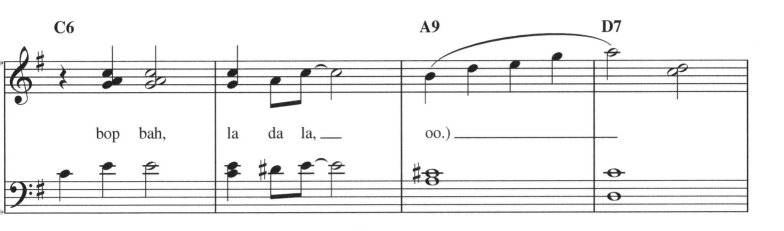

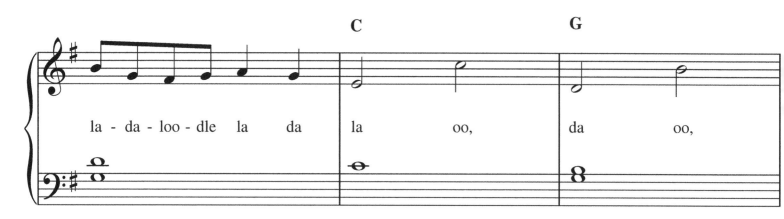

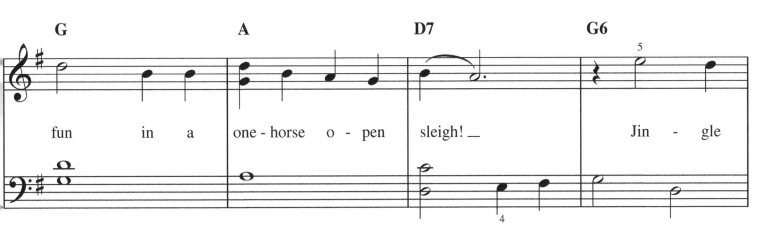

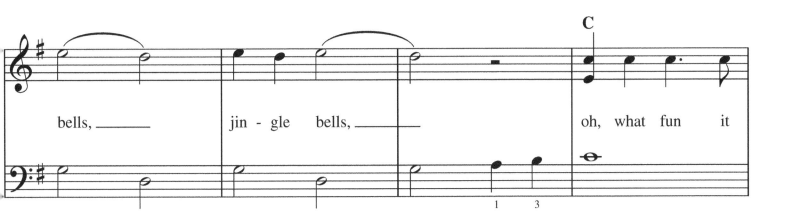

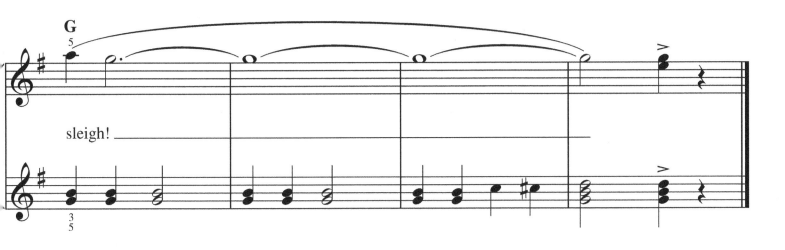

WHITE CHRISTMAS
from the Motion Picture Irving Berlin's HOLIDAY INN

Words and Music by
IRVING BERLIN

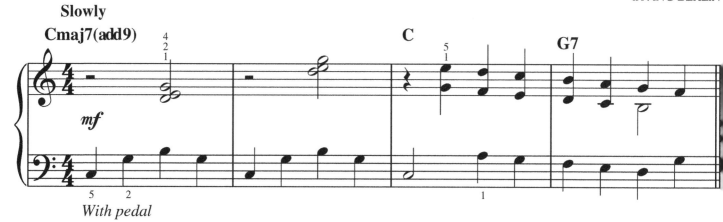

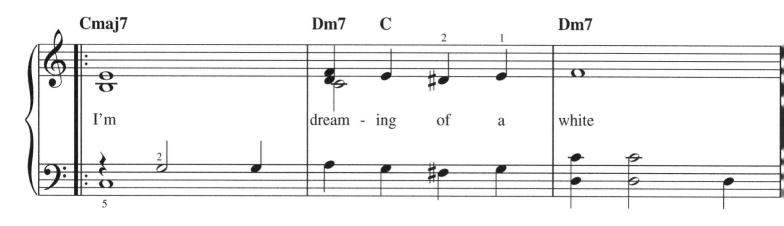

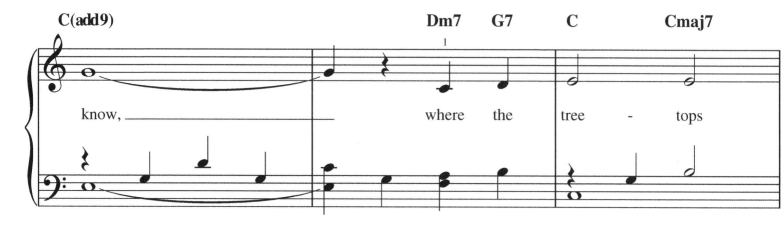

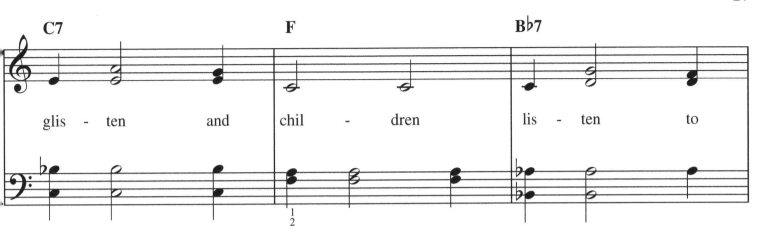

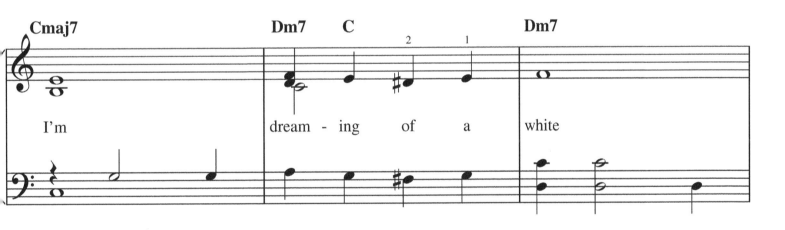

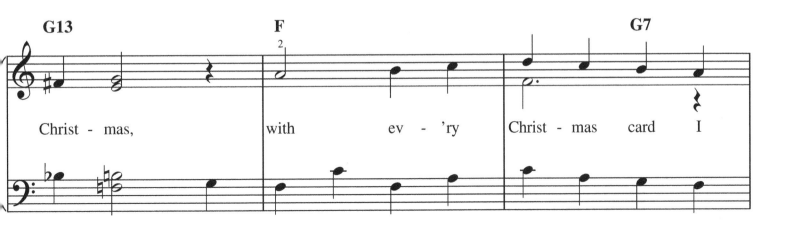

C(add9) · Dm7 · G7 · C · Cmaj7 · C7

write: _____ "May your days be mer - ry and

Fmaj(add9) · Fm · C · C#dim

bright _____ and may all your

Dm7 · G7 · **1.** · C · C(add9) · Dm7 · G7

Christ - mas - es be white."

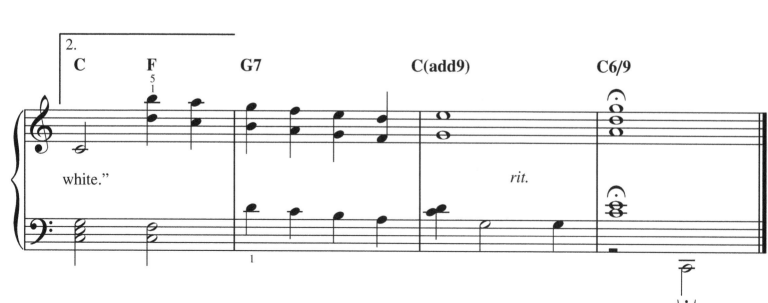

2. · C · F · G7 · C(add9) · C6/9

white."

rit.

All I WANT FOR CHRISTMAS IS YOU

Words and Music by MARIAH CAREY
and WALTER AFANASIEFF

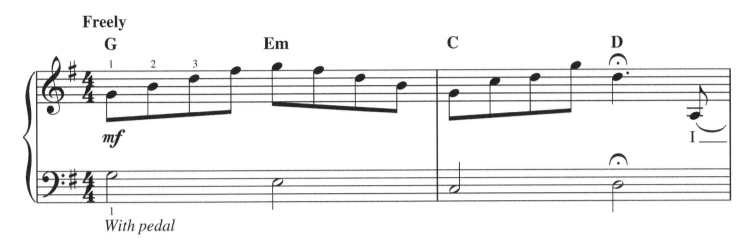

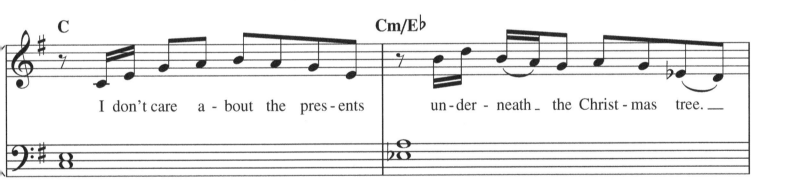

G/D   **E7**   **Am7**   **D7**

Make my wish come true: __ all I __ want for Christ-mas is you. __

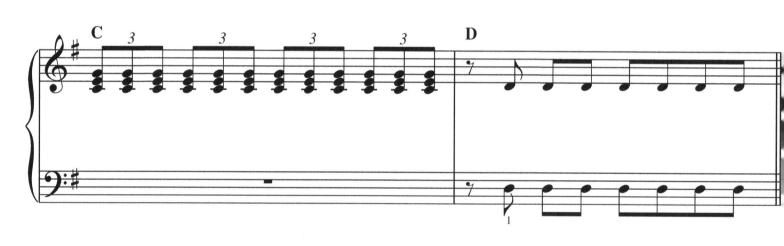

Moderately (♫ = ♩♪)

G   **Em**

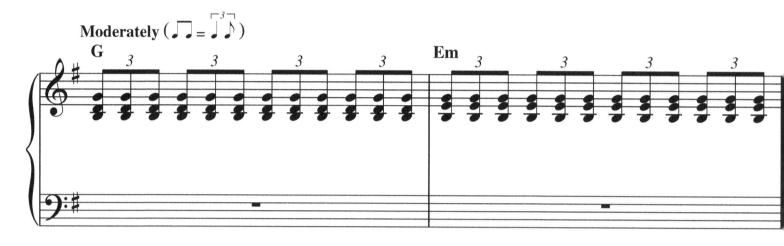

C   **D**

G

I don't want a lot __ for Christ-mas, there is just one thing __

I won't ask for much __ this Christ-mas, I won't e-ven wish __

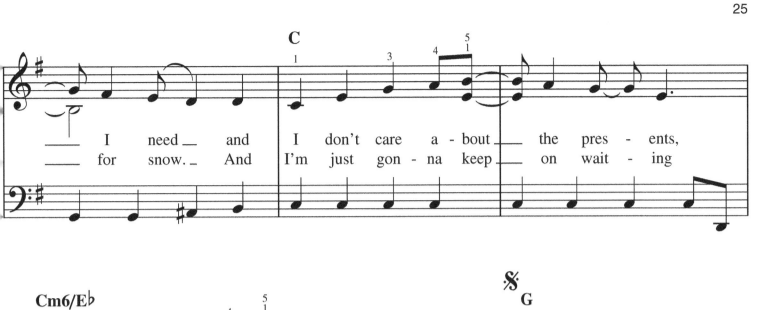

- mas day. ___
- deer click. ___
___ my door. ___

I just want you for ___ my own, ___
I just want you here ___ to - night, ___
I just want him for ___ my own; ___

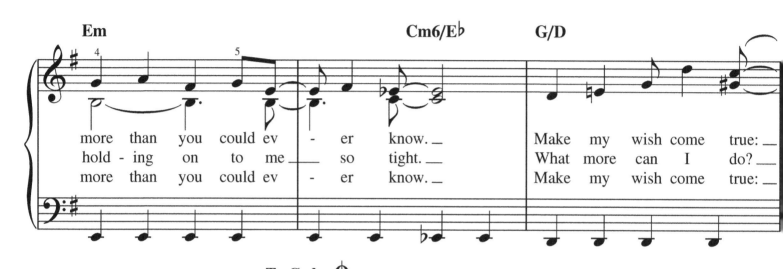

more than you could ev - er know. ___
hold - ing on to me ___ so tight. ___
more than you could ev - er know. ___

Make my wish come true: ___
What more can I do? ___
Make my wish come true: ___

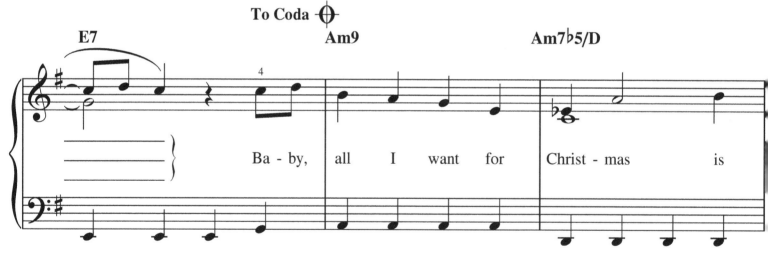

To Coda

Ba - by, all I want for Christ - mas is

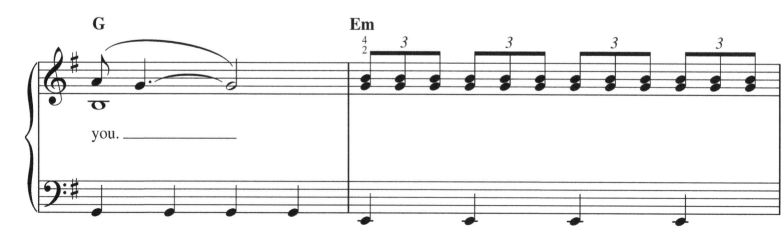

you. ___

27

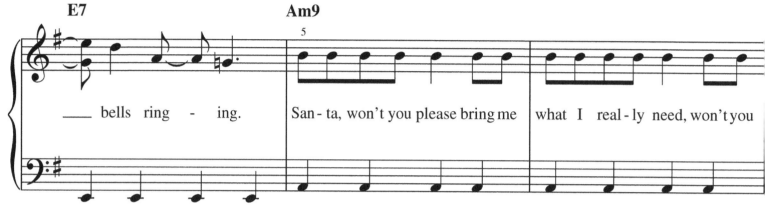

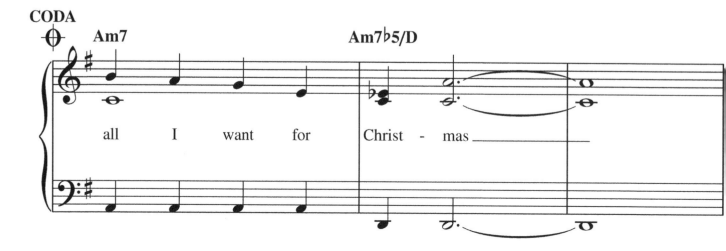

A HOLLY JOLLY CHRISTMAS

Music and Lyrics by
JOHNNY MARKS

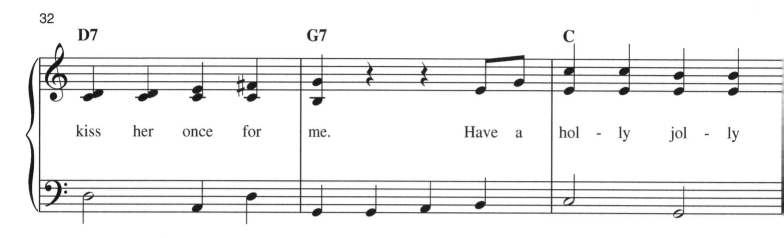

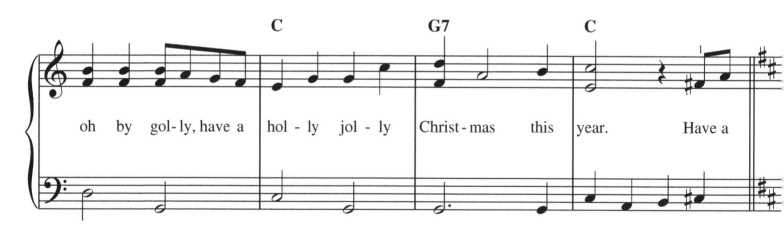

I don't know if there'll be snow, but let's all give a

cheer. Have a hol - ly jol - ly Christ - mas, and when you walk down the

street, say hel - lo to friends you know and

ev - 'ry - one you meet. Oh, ho, the

34

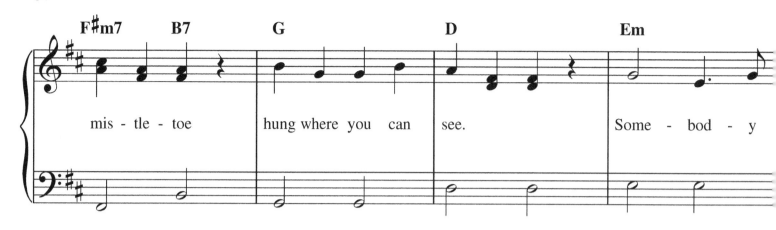

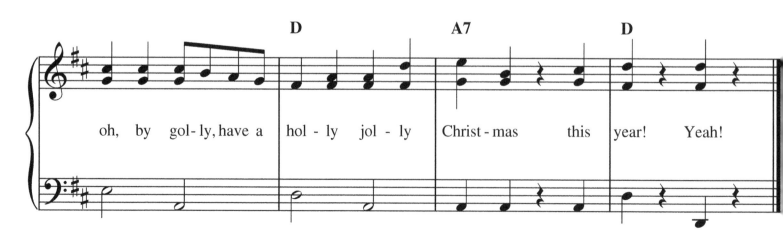

SANTA BABY

By JOAN JAVITS, PHIL SPRINGER
and TONY SPRINGER

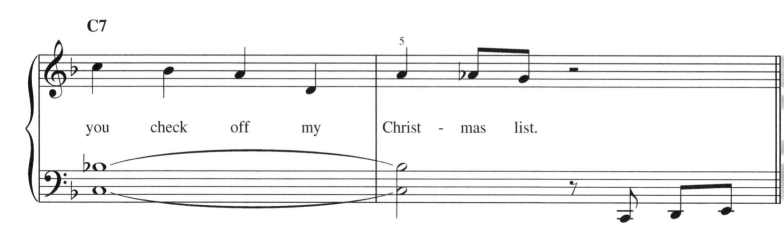

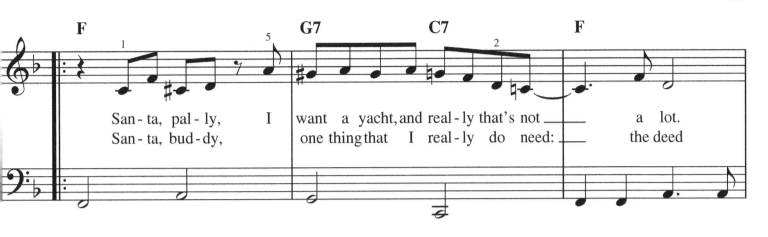

San - ta, pal - ly, I want a yacht, and real - ly that's not ____ a lot.
San - ta, bud - dy, one thing that I real - ly do need: ____ the deed

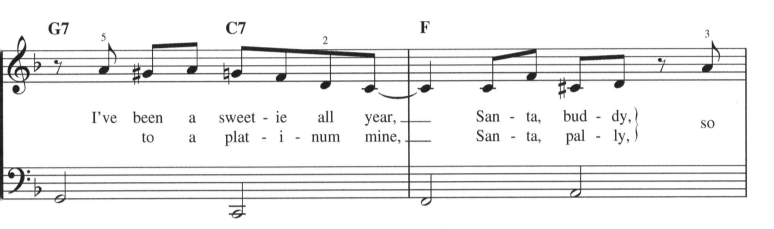

I've been a sweet - ie all year, ___ San - ta, bud - dy, ⎫ so
to a plat - i - num mine, ___ San - ta, pal - ly, ⎭

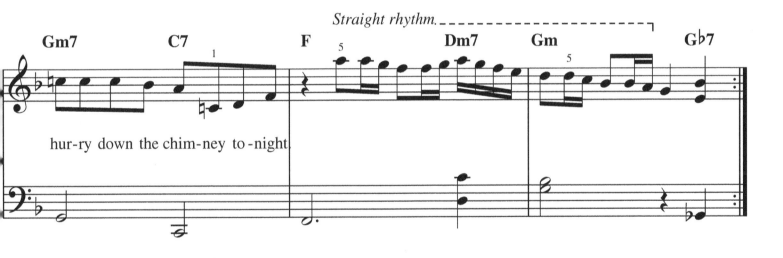

hur - ry down the chim - ney to - night.

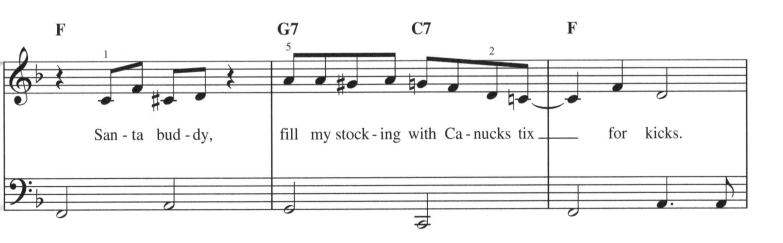

San - ta bud - dy, fill my stock - ing with Ca - nucks tix ___ for kicks.

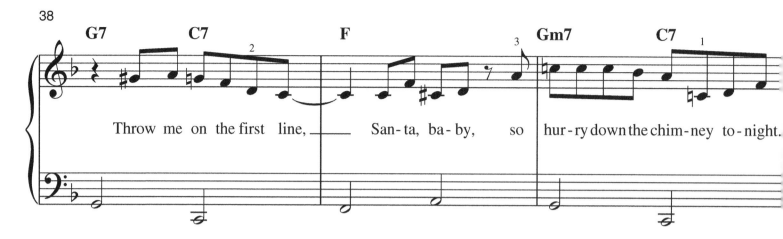

Throw me on the first line,___ San- ta, ba- by, so hur- ry down the chim- ney to- night.

Come and trim my

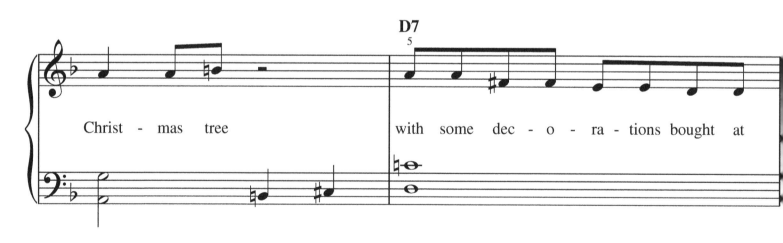

Christ - mas tree with some dec - o - ra - tions bought at

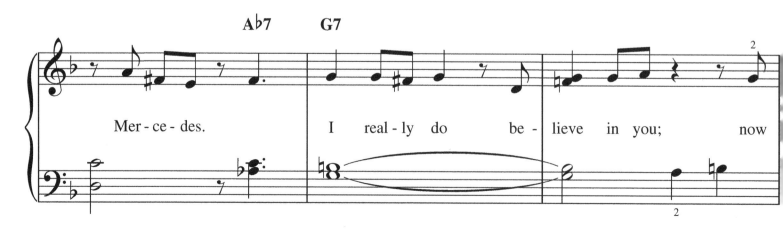

Mer - ce - des. I real - ly do be - lieve in you; now

let's see if you be-lieve in me. San-ta, pop-py, for-

got to men-tion one lit-tle thing: __ ch - ching. No, I don't mean as a loan, __

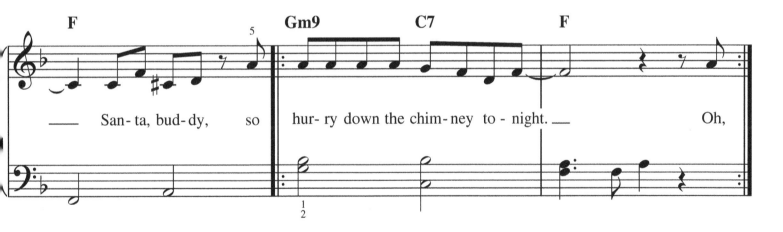

__ San-ta, bud-dy, so hur-ry down the chim-ney to-night. __ Oh,

hur - ry down the chim - ney to - night. __

HAVE YOURSELF A MERRY LITTLE CHRISTMAS

Words and Music by HUGH MARTIN
and RALPH BLANE

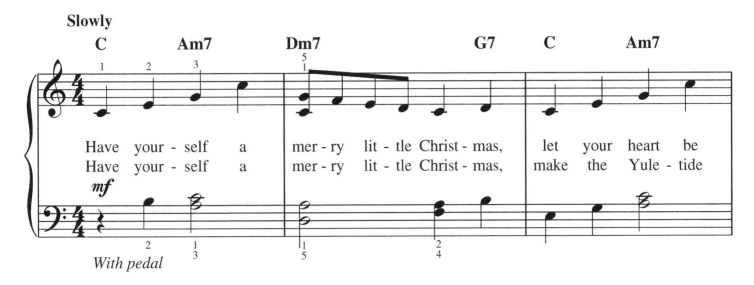

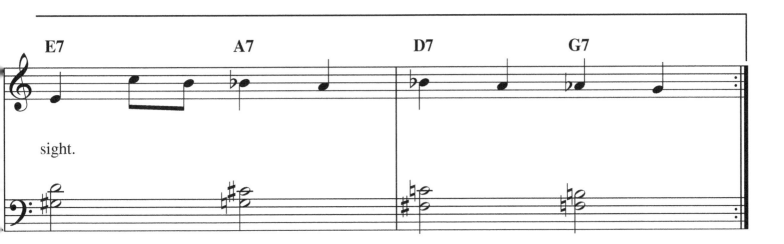

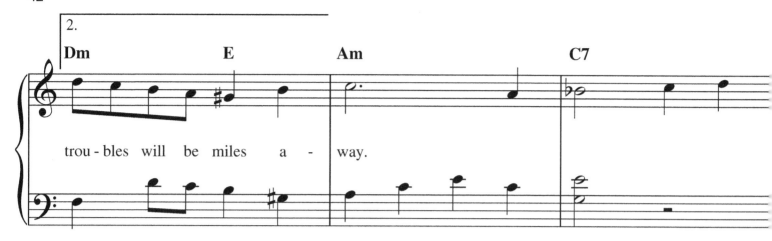

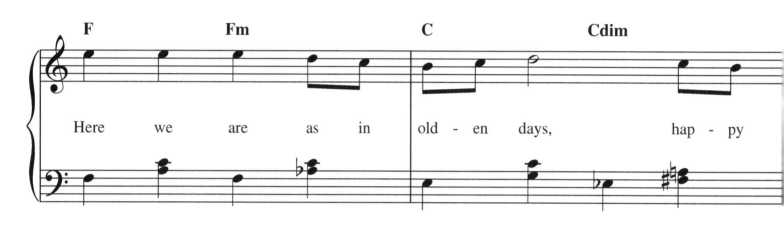

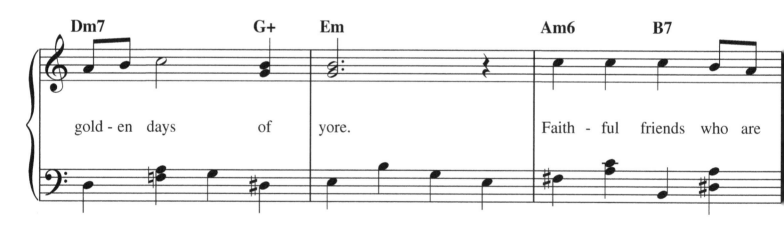

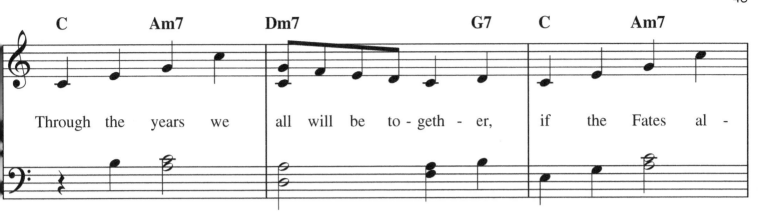

Through the years we all will be to - geth - er, if the Fates al -

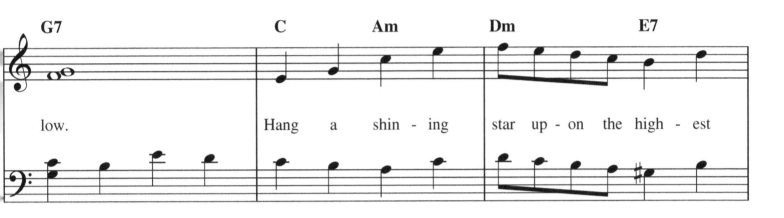

low. Hang a shin - ing star up - on the high - est

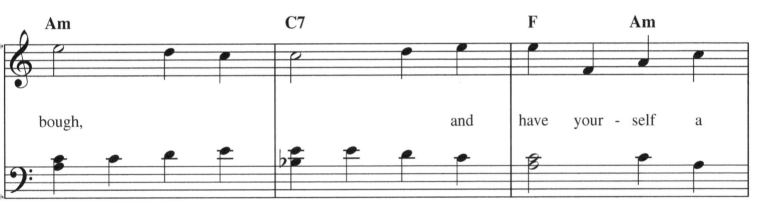

bough, and have your - self a

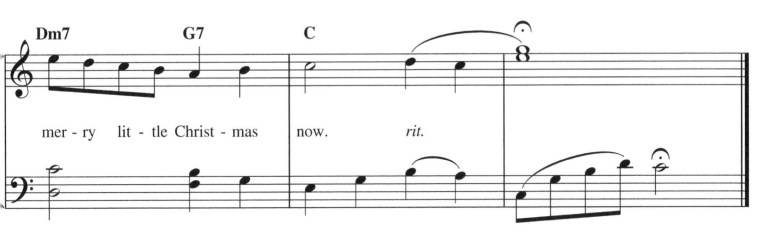

mer - ry lit - tle Christ - mas now. *rit.*

CHRISTMAS
(Baby Please Come Home)

Words and Music by PHIL SPECTOR,
ELLIE GREENWICH and JEFF BARRY

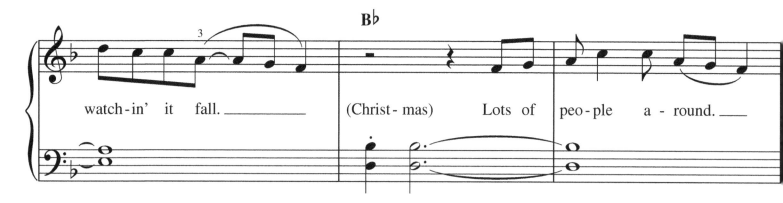

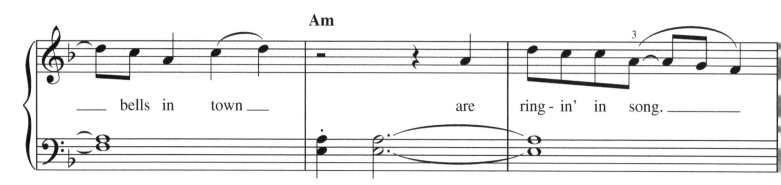

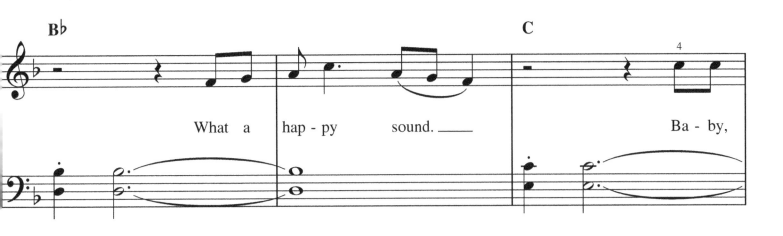

What a hap-py sound. ____ Ba - by,

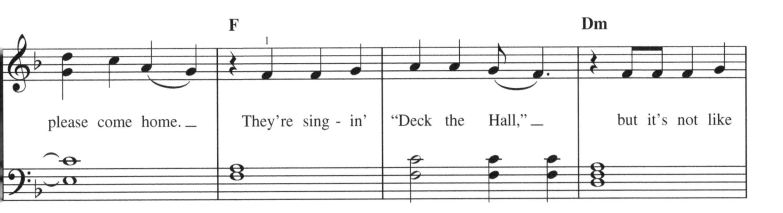

please come home. _ They're sing - in' "Deck the Hall," _ but it's not like

Christ-mas at all. _____ I re-mem-ber when you were here _

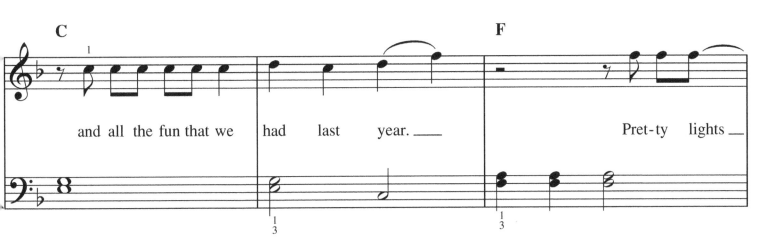

and all the fun that we had last year. ____ Pret-ty lights _

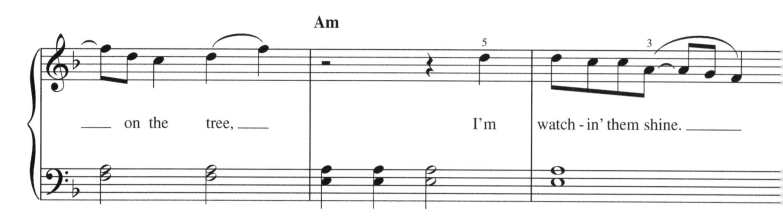

Am

____ on the tree, ____ I'm watch - in' them shine. _____

B♭ **C**

You should be here with me. ____ Ba - by,

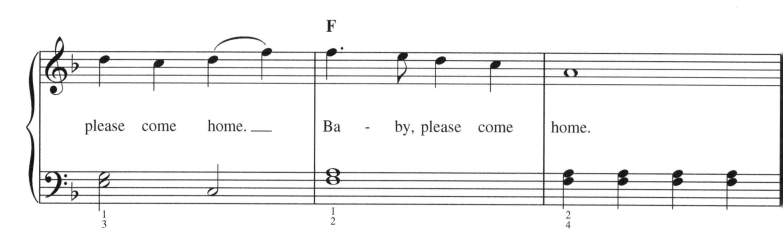

F

please come home. __ Ba - by, please come home.

Am **Am7** **B♭**

Ba - by, please come home,

I re-mem-ber when you were here ___ and all the fun that we

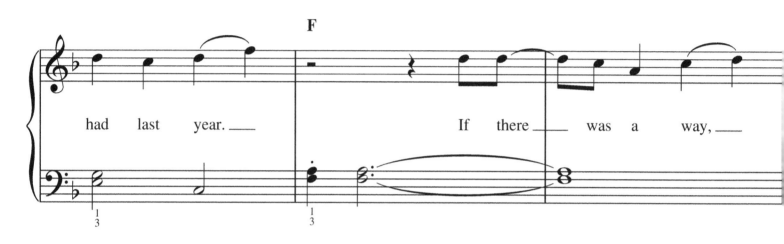

had last year. ___ If there ___ was a way, ___

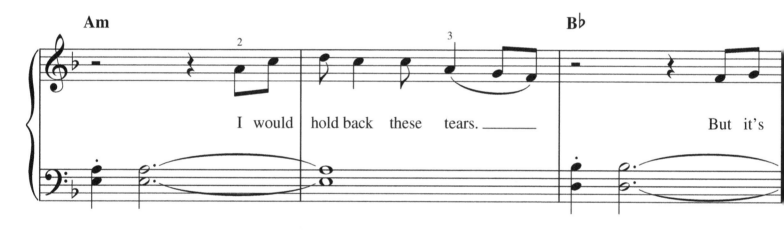

I would hold back these tears. ___ But it's

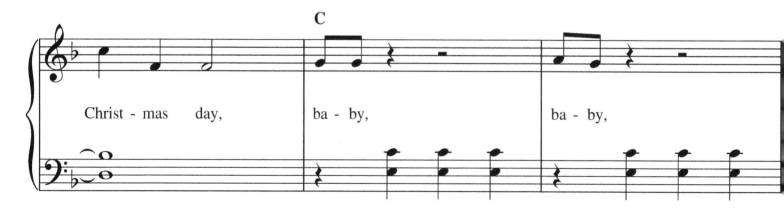

Christ-mas day, ba-by, ba-by,

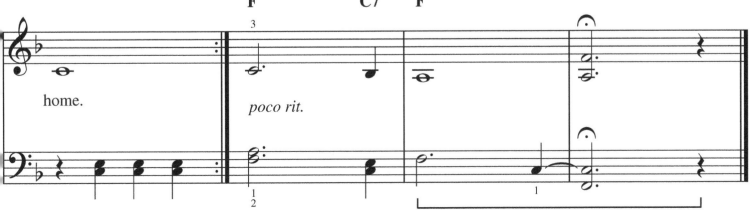

SILENT NIGHT

Traditional
Arranged by DAVID FOSTER

'round   yon   vir   -   gin   moth – er and   child.

Ho   –   ly   in – fant so   ten - der ___ and   mild,

To Coda

sleep   in   heav – en - ly   peace. _____

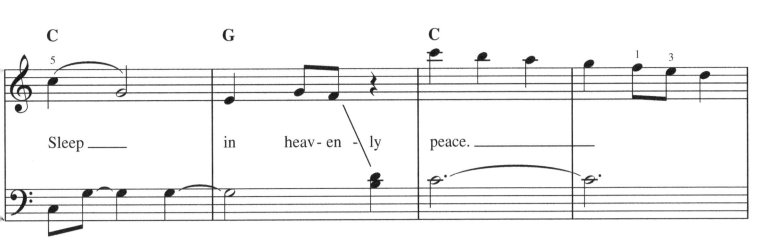

Sleep _____   in   heav - en - ly   peace. _____

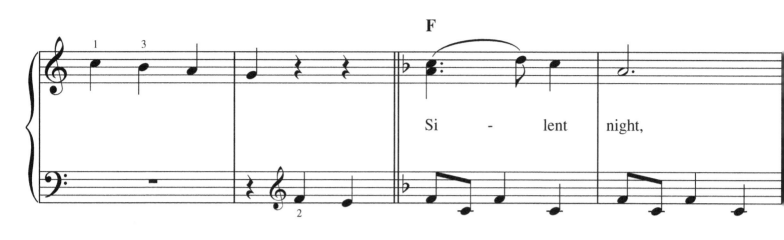

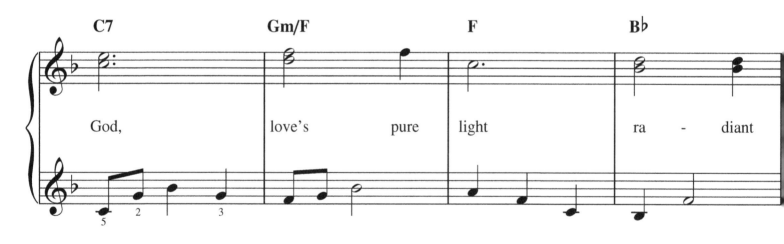

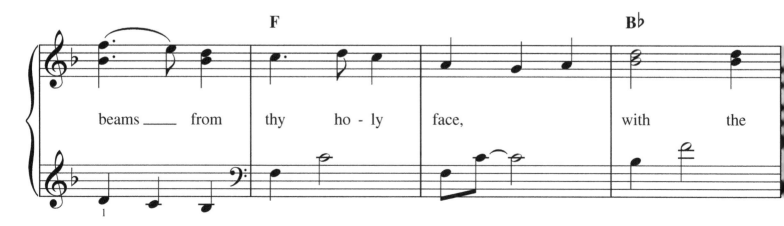

dawn   of re - deem -   ing   grace.

Je - sus,   Lord,   at thy   birth. _____

Je - sus,   Lord,   at thy   birth.

D.S. al Coda

CODA

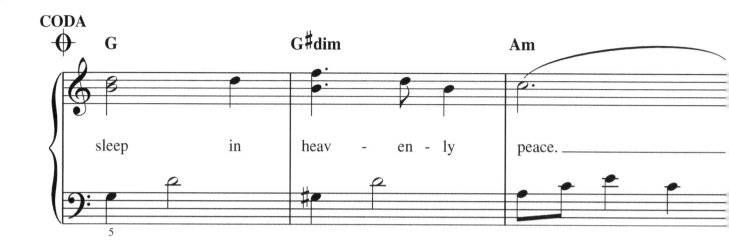

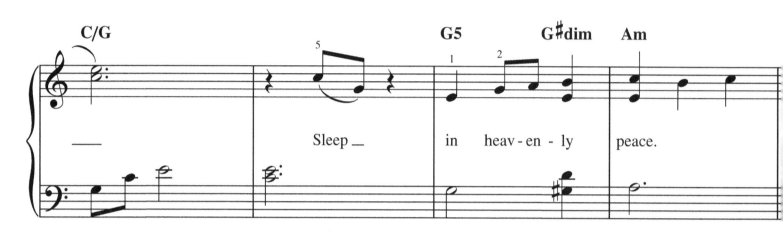

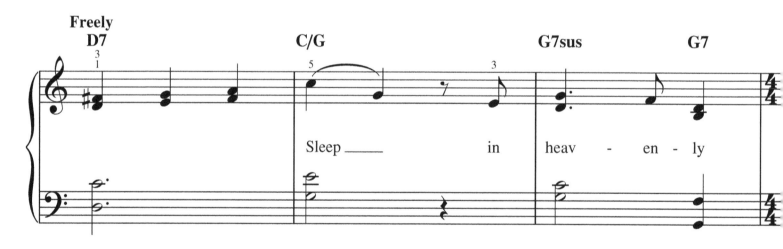

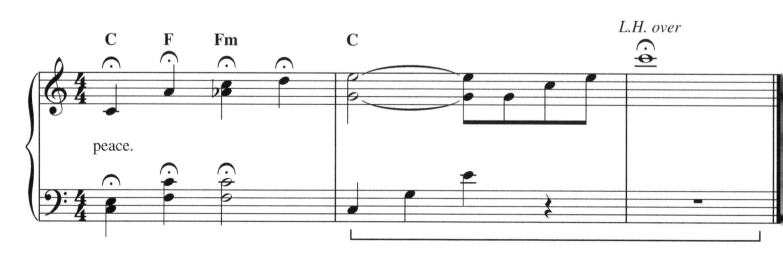

BLUE CHRISTMAS

Words and Music by BILLY HAYES
and JAY JOHNSON

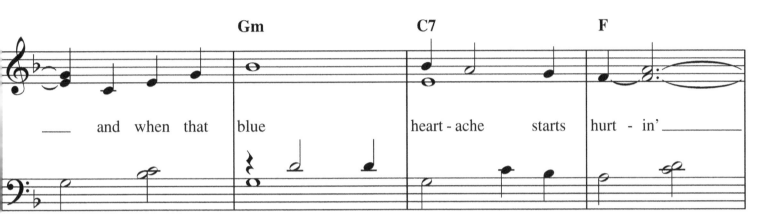

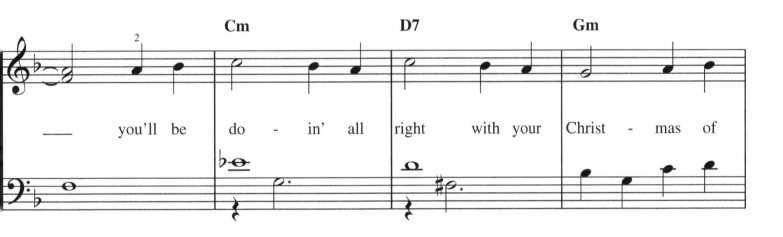

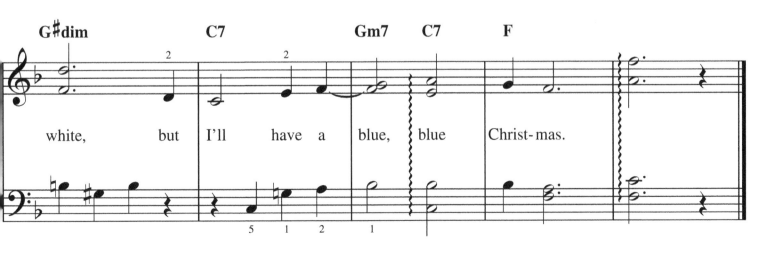

COLD DECEMBER NIGHT

Words and Music by MICHAEL BUBLÉ
ALAN CHANG and ROBERT ROCK

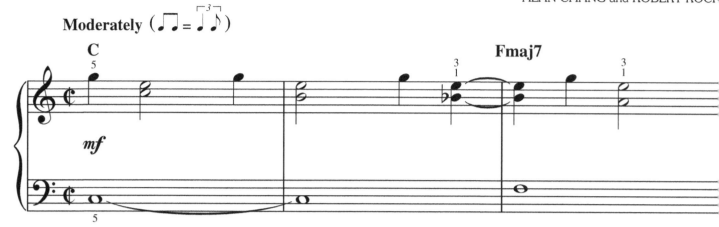

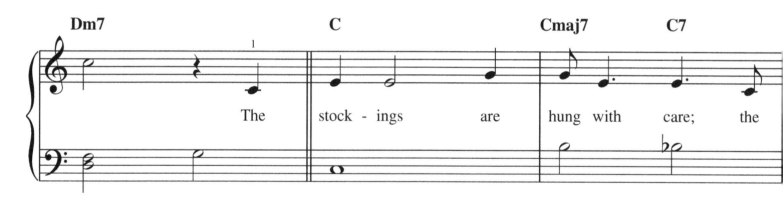

The stock-ings are hung with care; the chil-dren sleep with one eye o - pen.

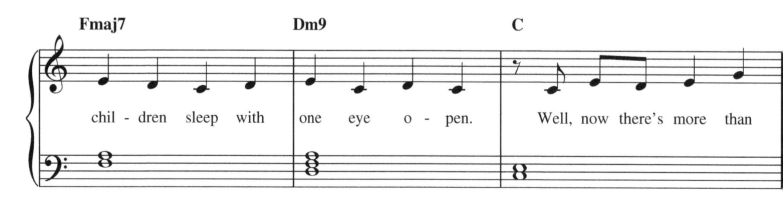

Well, now there's more than

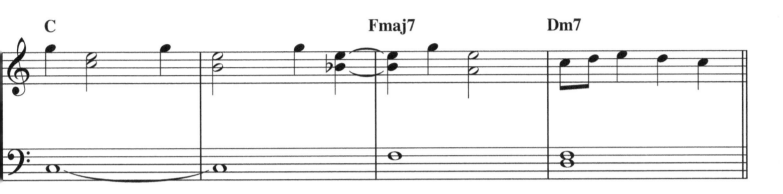

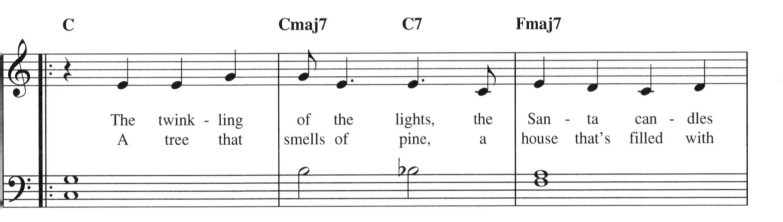

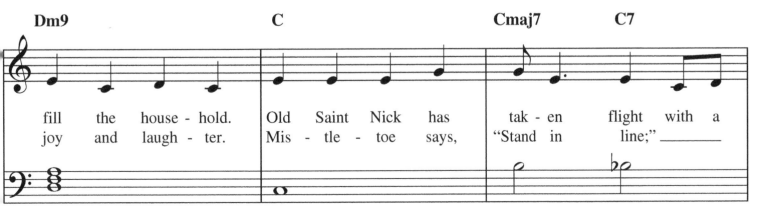

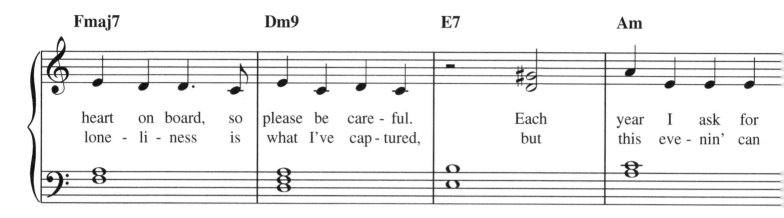

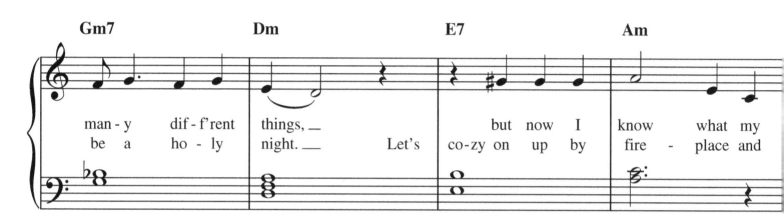

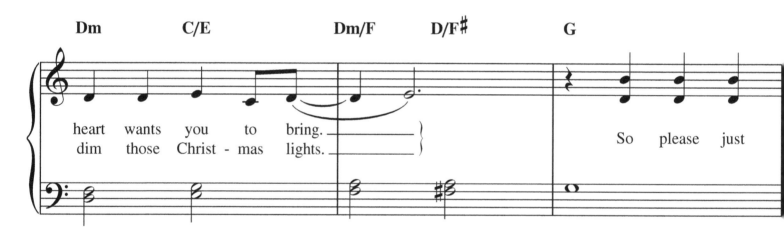

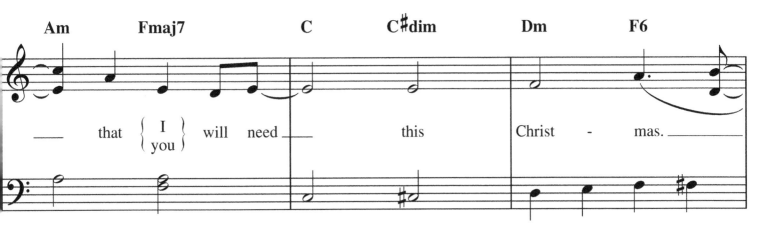

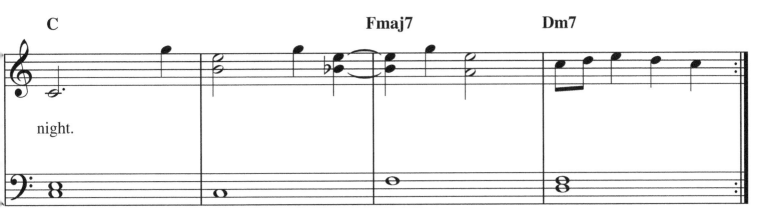

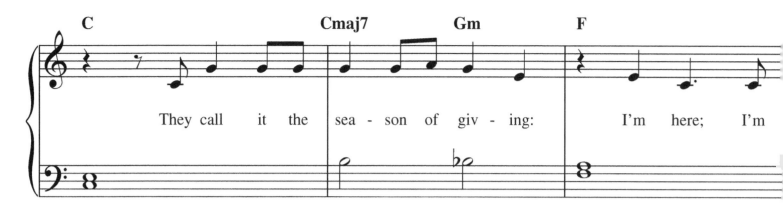

They call it the sea - son of giv - ing: I'm here; I'm

yours for the tak - ing. They call it the sea - son of giv - ing:

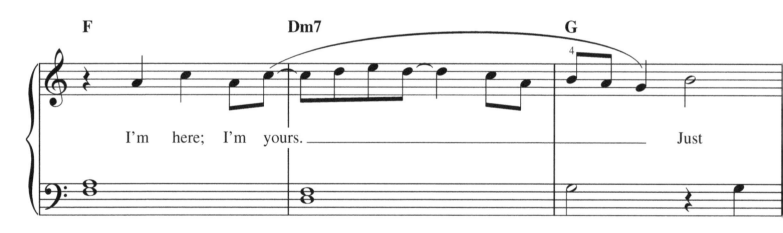

I'm here; I'm yours. _____ Just

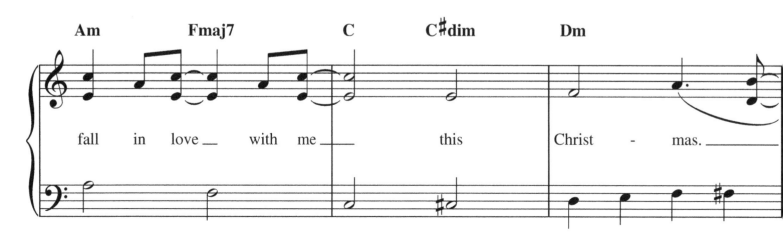

fall in love __ with me __ this Christ - mas. _____

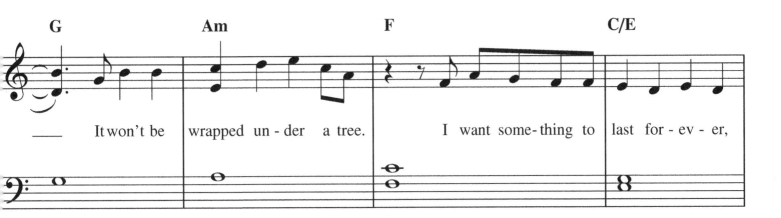

last for - ev - er, so kiss me on this cold De - cem - ber night.

They call it the

sea - son of giv - ing: I'm here, yours for the tak - ing. They call it the

sea - son of giv - ing: I'm here; I'm yours.

rit.

I'LL BE HOME FOR CHRISTMAS

Words and Music by KIM GANNON
and WALTER KENT

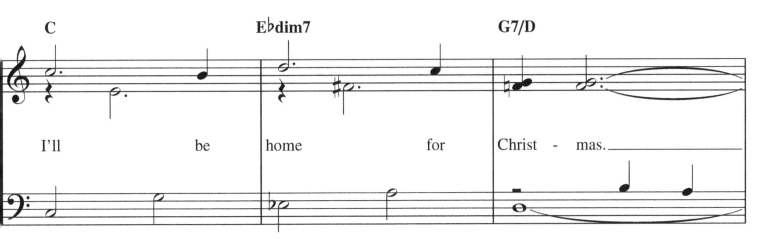

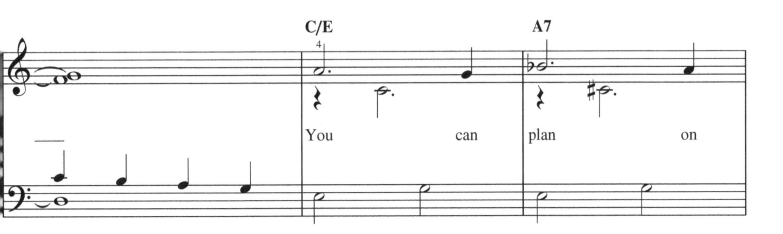

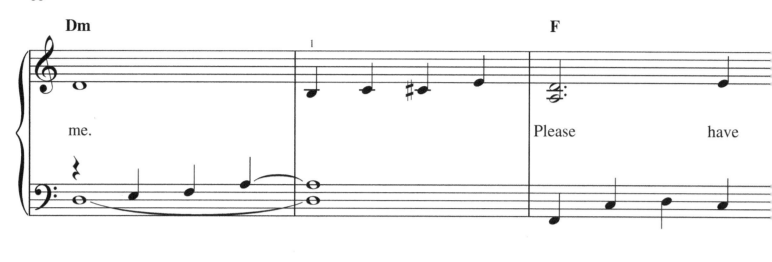

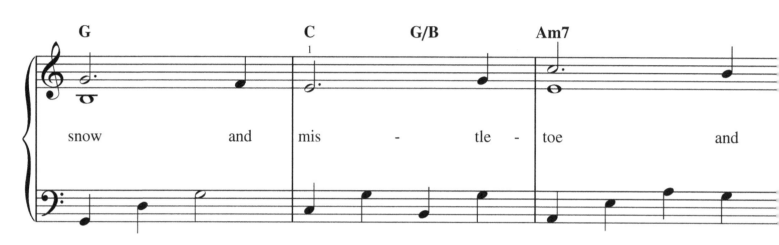

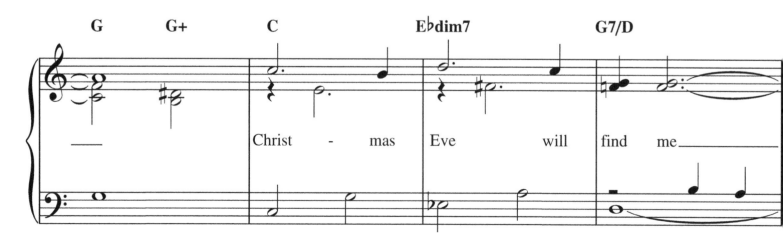

AVE MARIA

Traditional
Arranged by DAVID FOSTER

Slowly, with expression

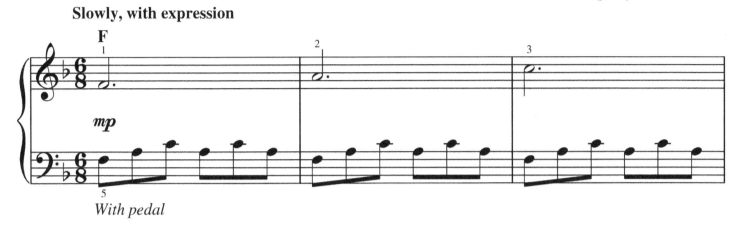

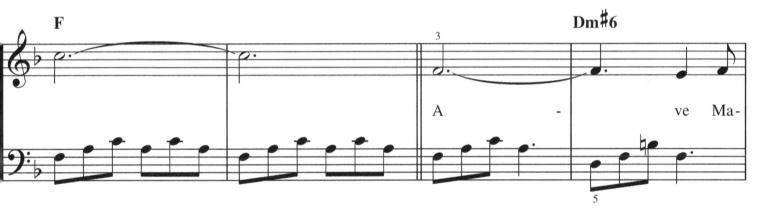

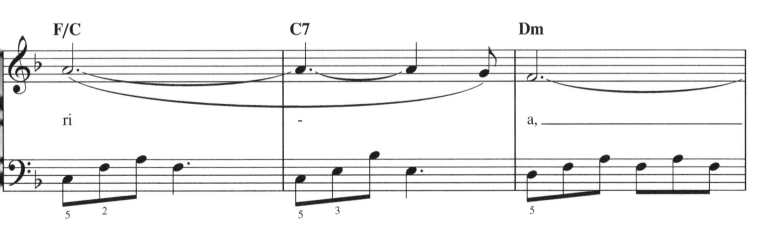

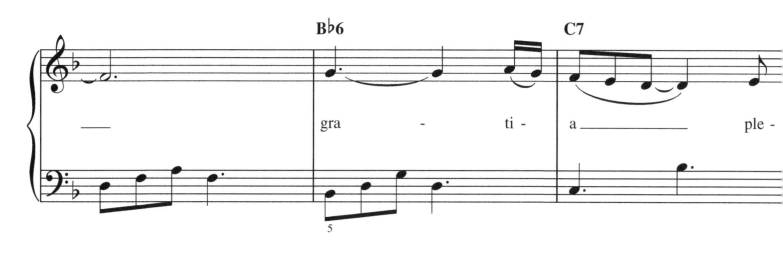

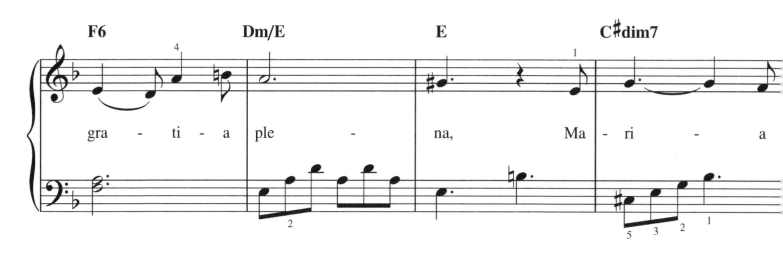

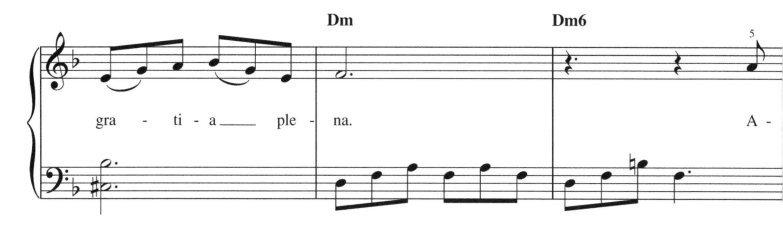

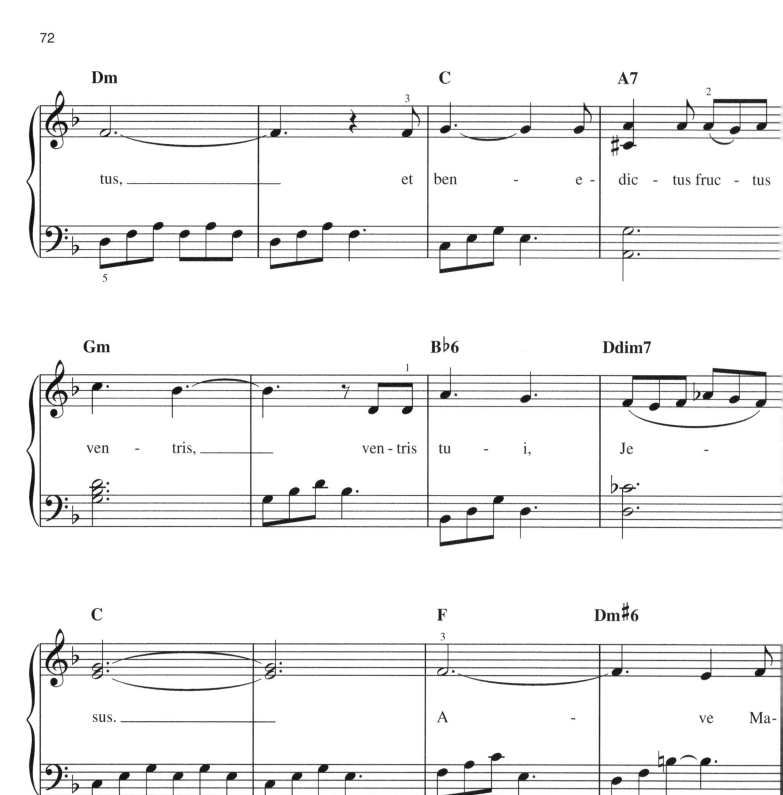

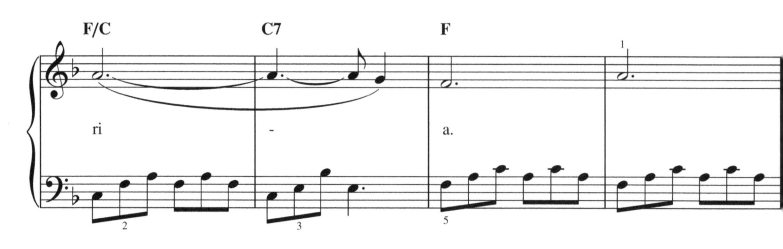

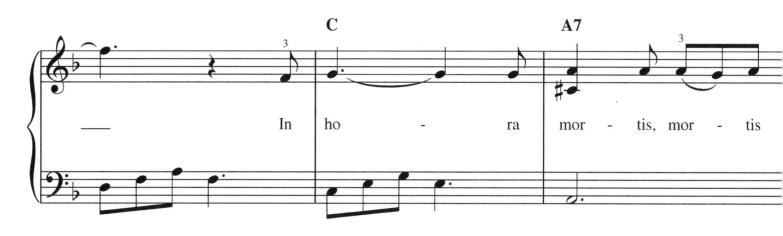

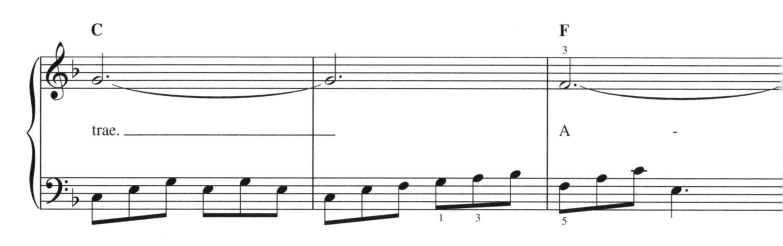

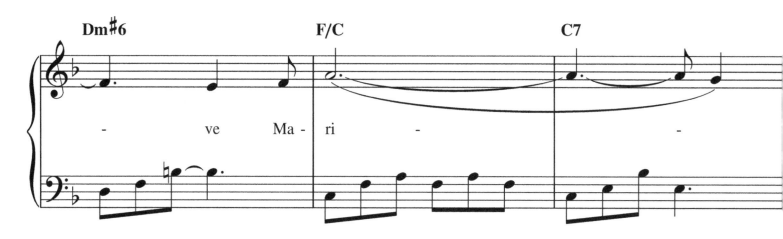

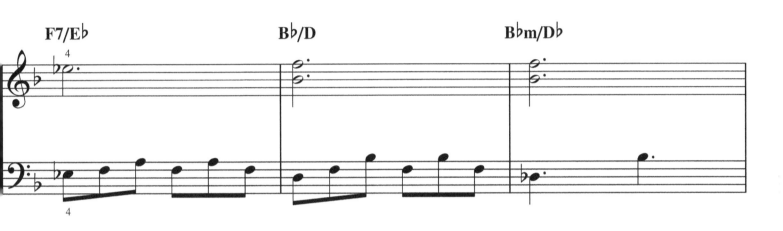

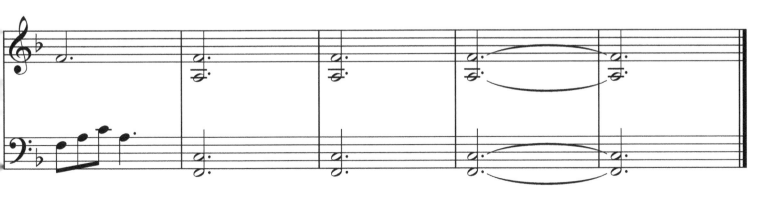

FELIZ NAVIDAD

Music and Lyrics by
JOSÉ FELICIANO

Moderately

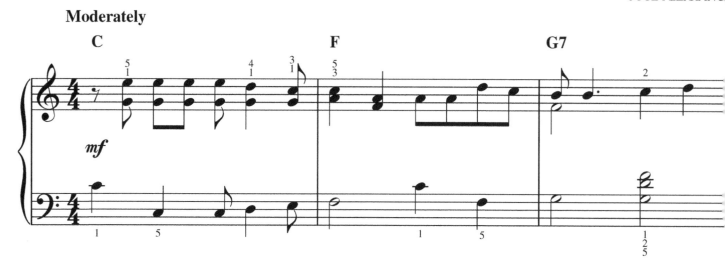

Fe - liz   Na - vi - dad. ____

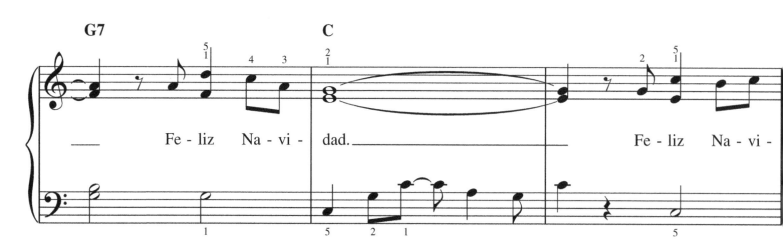

____ Fe - liz   Na - vi - dad. ____   Fe - liz   Na - vi -